B
B

Brighton Books
Nashville, TN

A JOURNEY
with
GOD
BEYOND
GRIEF

A JOURNEY *with* GOD BEYOND GRIEF

BY DR. CRISWELL FREEMAN, PSYD

BRIGHTON BOOKS
Nashville, TN 37204

ISBN 1-58334-127-7

The quoted ideas expressed in this book (but not scripture verses) are not, in all cases, exact quotations, as some have been edited for clarity and brevity. In all cases, the author has attempted to maintain the speaker's original intent. In some cases, quoted material for this book was obtained from secondary sources, primarily print media. While every effort was made to ensure the accuracy of these sources, the accuracy cannot be guaranteed. For additions, deletions, corrections or clarifications in future editions of this text, please write BRIGHTON BOOKS.

Certain passages of this text have been excerpted from the book: *Your Grief and God's Promises*, written by Criswell Freenam and published by Walnut Grove Press ©1999, used with permission.

Scripture taken from the HOLY BIBLE, NEW INTERNATIONAL VERSION ©. NIV ©. Copyright © 1973, 1978, 1984, by International Bible Society. Used by permission of Zondervan Publishing House. All rights reserved.

Scripture taken from *THE MESSAGE*. Copyright © 1993, 1994, 1995, 1996. Used by permission of NavPress Publishing Group.

Scripture taken from the NEW AMERICAN STANDARD BIBLE®, Copyright © 1960, 1962, 1963, 1968, 1971, 1972, 1973, 1975, 1977, 1995 by The Lockman Foundation. Used by permission.

Scripture quotations marked (NLT) are taken from The Holy Bible, New Living Translation, Copyright © 1996. Used by permission of Tyndale House Publishers, Incorporated, Wheaton, Illinois 60189. All rights reserved.

Printed in the United States of America
Cover Design & Page Layout: *Bart Dawson*
Cover Photograph: *Neal & Molly Jansen/Superstock*

1 2 3 4 5 6 7 8 9 10 • 02 03 04 05 06 07 08 09 10

Acknowledgments: The author wishes to acknowledge the help and support of the following men and women, all of whom contributed greatly to this text: Angela Freeman, Dick and Mary Freeman, Wayne Oates, Mark Stone, Bob Powers, Jim Gallery, and Ron Smith. The author also wishes to thank the creative and generous staff at Brighton Books.

FOR ALL WHO MOURN

TABLE OF CONTENTS

INTRODUCTION

Weeping may endure for a night,
but joy cometh in the morning.
—

Psalm 30:5 KJV

I n the course of a lifetime, grief visits each of us. We experience a deeply significant loss: perhaps the death of a loved one or the loss of health; perhaps divorce or the disintegration of a personal relationship; perhaps the loss of a job or a significant financial reversal. Whatever its cause, grief surrounds us with a pain so intense and so profound that we fear we can never recover. But with God's help, we can recover.

The Christian faith, as communicated through the Holy Bible, is a healing faith. God offers comfort through His Word, through His Spirit, through His church, and, above all, through His Son Jesus Christ. God promises us that even if our lives are forever changed by a tragedy beyond words, He will comfort us. In times of trouble, God offers courage. In times of hopelessness, He offers assurance. In times of desperation, God offers restoration to those who place their trust in Him.

For Christians, grief need never be a permanent condition. To the contrary, the grieving process can be a journey—with God—through and beyond the pain. Even when we suffer mightily, even when we fear that every ounce of strength is gone, God remains steadfast. For Christians, the grave is not a final resting place; it is a place of rebirth. For believers, God is never absent. He continues to manifest His plan in good times and bad.

If you are experiencing the intense pain of a recent loss, or if you are continuing to mourn a loss from long ago, this book is intended to help. This collection of verses, quotations, and brief commentaries is intended to provide you with an understanding of the grieving process. It is also intended to give you clear and unambiguous hope for the future.

Loss and grief are inevitable consequences of life. Grief, like other challenges, is best faced head-on; it should not be repressed, avoided, or feared. Instead, bereavement should be worked through—and walked through—in partnership with God. If this book, in some small way, assists you as you journey through and beyond your pain, it will have served its purpose. May God bless you and keep you, and may He place his healing hand upon your heart today and forever.

— Criswell Freeman

Chapter 1

A TIME TO GRIEVE

I am weary of my crying: my throat is dried:
mine eyes fail while I wait for my God.

—

Psalm 69:3 KJV

Grief is a profound and personal experience, but it is also a universal experience, a journey that has been clearly mapped by those who have documented the common elements of human suffering. Grief can also be a spiritual journey, a time when wounded Christians gradually transform their suffering into deeper, more intimate relationships with God. But, in the beginning, grief seems less like a spiritual journey than a spiritual test. Often, that test begins with a period of numbness and shock.

When we suffer an unexpected loss—or the emotional impact of an expected loss—grief often begins with odd, almost surreal feelings of disbelief, foggy sensations that seem to say, "This can't really be happening," or, "This must be a bad dream." Over time, the emotional fog lifts, and a painful period of grieving begins. If we work through that pain, and, if the grieving process takes its normal course, then we gradually begin to regain emotional balance as the pain begins to fade. Eventually, a new life is raised from the ashes of the old.

Christians face grief armed with God's promises. Throughout the Holy Bible, God promises to comfort and heal those who call upon Him. The Psalmist writes, *Then they cried unto the LORD in their trouble, and he saved them out of their distresses. (Psalm 107:13 KJV)* Just as God restored His people in Old-Testament times, so does He protect His children of every generation—and so will He protect you.

As you experience the searing pain of any significant loss, knowledge is power. The more you understand the grieving process, the better you can cope with its many twists and turns. But, whatever the nature of your loss and whatever the timetable of your healing, always remember this overriding truth: God is with you; God is good; and you are protected. The words of Psalm 34 make this promise: *The Lord is close to the brokenhearted and saves those who are crushed in spirit. (Psalm 34:18 NIV)* Upon this promise, grieving Christians can—and must—depend.

CHARACTERISTICS OF THE GRIEVING PROCESS

While no single formula can adequately describe the grieving process for every circumstance or for every individual, experts *have* described the following stages of bereavement. If you have experienced a profound loss, you can be encouraged by the knowledge that grief is a process that, although terribly painful, is also predictable in its course. The grieving process often includes the following progressive stages:

<u>A Brief Period of Shock</u>: This phase may be punctuated by intense feelings of fear, alarm, disbelief, or anger.

<u>A Brief Period of Numbness</u>: During this time, the individual may appear calm and unaffected.

<u>A Longer Period or Yearning, Searching, and Intense Sadness</u>: This phase may last months or even years. During this time, the bereaved person endures periods of despair, disorganization, interrupted sleep, periodic bouts of anxiety, and fear for the future. Such feelings, although painful, are normal symptoms of the grieving process.

<u>Reorganization and Recovery</u>: Gradually, as the mourner adjusts to the reality of a changed world, grief gives way to cherished memories, a sense of acceptance, and hope for the future.

Obviously, the timing of the above stages varies from individual to individual *and* according to the magnitude of each particular loss. It is also important to note that most mourners move back and forth between stages as they gradually progress toward reorganization and recovery. Unfortunately, there are no hard-and-fast time-tables. Still, mourners can be comforted in the knowledge that, in time, healing is the natural and expected prognosis for those who grieve.

Grief is the aftermath of any
       deeply significant loss.

Wayne Oates

When the full impact of our loss hit home,
       it seemed that everything moved
              in slow motion.

Zig Ziglar

O Lord God of my salvation,
   I have cried day and night before thee...
       for my soul is full of troubles....

Psalm: 88:1-3 KJV

God of our life, there are days when
the burdens we carry chafe our shoulders
and weigh us down; when the road
seems dreary and endless, the skies grey
and threatening; when our lives have
no music in them, and our hearts are lonely,
and our souls have lost their courage.
Flood the path with light, run our eyes
to where the skies are full of promise;
tune our hearts to brave music; give us
the sense of comradeship with heroes
and saints of every age; and so quicken our
spirits that we may be able to encourage
the souls of all who journey with us on
the road of life, to Your honour and glory.

St. Augustine

...Be not afraid, only believe.

Mark 5:36 KJV

There are no crown wearers in heaven
who were not cross bearers here below.

C. H. Spurgeon

Even in the winter, even in the midst of
the storm, the sun is still there. Somewhere,
up above the clouds, it still shines and warms
and pulls at the life buried deep inside
the brown branches and frozen earth.
The sun is there! Spring will come.

Gloria Gaither

God has never promised to keep us immune
from trouble. He says,
"I will be with you in trouble."

Oswald Chambers

Grief affects us spiritually, physically,
   socially, and in every other facet of life.

Zig Ziglar

Trouble and anguish have taken hold on me:
   yet thy commandments are my delights.

Psalm 119:143 KJV

We must through much tribulation
   enter into the kingdom of heaven.

Acts 14:22 KJV

Jesus does not say,
"There is no storm." He says,
"I am here, do not toss but trust."

—

Vance Havner

For the eyes of the Lord range throughout
  the earth to strengthen those whose hearts
    are fully committed to him.

II Chronicles 16:9 NIV

Fear thou not; for I am with thee.

Isaiah 41:10 KJV

...Be strong and courageous.
  Do not be terrified; do not be discouraged,
    for the Lord your God will be with you
      wherever you go.

Joshua 1: 9-10 NIV

I am not alone, because the Father is with me.

John 16:32 KJV

29

God whispers to us in our pleasures,
speaks in our conscience,
but shouts in our pain.

C. S. Lewis

I will be your God throughout your lifetime—
until your hair is white with age.
I made you, and I will care for you.
I will carry you along and save you.

Isaiah 46:4 NLT

Nevertheless God, that comforteth those
that are cast down, comforted us....

II Corinthians 7:6 KJV

You cannot overcome if there is
nothing to overcome.

Oswald Chambers

For therein is the righteousness of God
revealed from faith to faith: as it is written,
The just shall live by faith.

Romans 1:17 KJV

"Lord Help!" they cried in their trouble,
and he saved them from their distress.

Psalm 107:28 NLT

God shall wipe away
all the tears from their eyes.

—

Revelation: 7:17 KJV

Chapter 2

EXPRESSING YOUR EMOTIONS

I have heard your prayer,
I have seen your tears;
behold, I will heal you....
—

II Kings 20:5 RSV

W hen a loved one dies, some Christians find it difficult to grieve. After all, they say to themselves, God's Word promises eternal life for those who die in Christ, and God's plan for the world is perfect. Why, then, can there be any reason for sadness? So instead of expressing appropriate sorrow for what is lost, some Christians steadfastly refuse to allow themselves permission to grieve.

God gave us emotions for a reason. When we express those emotions sincerely to our loved ones and to our God, we begin the process of healing. But, if we suppress our emotions or ignore them altogether, we may needlessly prolong our suffering.

Honest, heartfelt expressions of grief can, by their very nature, be painful to endure, so we tend to avoid them. We may pretend that "everything is okay" when it is not. Or we may tell ourselves that "it is not right to feel sad" when quite the opposite is true.

Appropriate expressions of sorrow help move us through and beyond the grieving process. If you have experienced a significant loss in your life, don't deny it; grieve it. Express your feelings.

Allow tears to flow. Share your sadness with others. Acknowledge your pain and tell your story. By honestly expressing your grief, you are taking an active role in God's plan for your recovery.

Tears are the natural form of release for
the still-suppressed feelings of love and
gratitude, and also for the reservoir of pain
and sorrow we have in our hearts.

Zig Ziglar

AVOIDING "NO-END GRIEF"

In his book *Your Particular Grief,* the pioneering pastoral counselor Wayne Oates writes about the phenomenon of "no-end grief," which he describes as "those griefs that have no particular time of conclusion." He includes in this category such events as divorce, major illness, and physical handicaps. Such situations, as Oates acknowledges, must be lived with. But, he also warns against allowing them to become the central focus of one's life. Oates writes, "The critical spiritual problem in the struggle against bitterness is this: You are being tempted to place a severe experience...at the center of your whole life. This is idolatry."

Grieving Christians are wise to express their sorrows to friends, relatives, pastors and counselors. The grieving process is vitally important and, at times, overwhelming for the bereaved. But, grief should never become the absolute center of a Christian's life—that place is reserved for God the Father and His only begotten Son.

If you fear that you may be slipping into a prolonged, "no-end" cycle of bitterness and personal destruction, remember that help is always near. First, take your burden to God in prayer. Then, call your pastor and set up a time to meet and discuss your situation in depth. You may also consider visiting an experienced grief counselor or, as an alternative, joining a self-help group that deals with your particular concern. Finally, consult your physician or a qualified professional counselor to gain a clear understanding of the difference between grief and depression (see appendix).

O Lord my God, I cried unto thee,
and thou hast healed me.

Psalm 30:2 KJV

O my God, my soul is cast down within me:
therefore I will remember thee....

Psalm 42:6 KJV

Ye shall be sorrowful, but your sorrow
shall be turned into joy.

John 16:20 KJV

A teardrop on earth summons
the King of heaven.

Charles Swindoll

Blessed are they that mourn: for they shall be comforted.

—

Matthew 5:4 KJV

He heals the brokenhearted
and binds their wounds.

—

Psalm 147: 3 NASB

A time to weep and a time to laugh;
   A time to mourn and a time to dance.

Ecclesiastes 3: 4 NASB

God has a bottle and a book for
   his people's tears. What was sown as
   a tear will come up as a pearl.

Matthew Henry

He restores my soul....

—

Psalm 23:3 NASB

Chapter 3

ANGER AND GUILT

Wise men turn away anger.

—

Proverbs 29:8 NASB

The experience of grief is often accompanied by emotions of anger, guilt and regret. We are understandably angry about our losses; we may feel guilty about the things that we could have done to prevent them; and we may have regrets about things left undone or unsaid. During times of profound loss, negative emotions are understandable and expected. But, we should beware: Prolonged feelings of anger, guilt, or regret have the potential to do us great harm.

Anger, left unchecked, tends to invade every aspect of life, eventually transforming itself into bitterness. Guilt and regret over past events that cannot be changed create an environment of self-doubt and self-recrimination. The need to avoid negative emotions is obvious, but the battle against them is never fully won in this lifetime, so we must be vigilant.

If your thoughts are dominated by feelings of anger, guilt, jealousy, fear, or, for that matter, any other negative emotion, understand that these emotions are part of the journey through and beyond grief. But, understand, too, that hurtful feelings should never become a permanent part of your emotional makeup. God has better things in store for you.

If your loved one is dead,
>   ask yourself this question:
>   Are you still angry at him?

Wayne Oates

Cease from anger and forsake wrath;
>   Do not fret; it leads only to evildoing.

Psalm 37:8 NASB

Whenever you stand praying, forgive,
>   if you have anything against anyone,
>   so that your Father in heaven will also
>   forgive you your transgressions.

Mark 11:25 NASB

CONTROLLING NEGATIVE EMOTIONS BEFORE THEY CONTROL US

Negative thought patterns are best snuffed out in their infancy; otherwise, they grow to become exaggerated, irrational, and repetitive. Furthermore, strong negative emotions seldom remain focused for long: What may begin as anger about a particular event or person can soon become generalized as we become angry with our world (and, unfortunately, with those closest to us). The results of negative, irrational thought patterns are predictably destructive. They sabotage our happiness, jeopardize our relationships, interrupt our sleep, and, most importantly, separate us from the healing love of God's Holy Spirit.

Thankfully, negative thinking is very often a matter of habit—and habits can be changed. If you find yourself beset with chronic episodes of negative, circular thinking, try the following:

1. Remember that your emotions are not beyond your control. To a great extent, you can control repetitive negative thoughts...and should.

2. Pay attention to your moods and look for triggers that send you spiraling into periods of

negativity. Then, the next time you encounter such a trigger, catch yourself before your negative emotions take a firm grip on you. Take a deep breath, relax, say a prayer, and calm yourself *before* your strong emotions reach the boiling point.

3. Keep a journal that contains your thoughts *and* a record of the things that tend to upset you. As you write in your journal, do not minimize your feelings of loss and bitterness, *but* do not ignore your resources, either.

4. Be on guard against perfectionism: The world is not perfect, and neither are your loved ones. To expect perfection from others (or from yourself) is to set yourself up for continual disappointment.

5. You may find yourself more depressed in the darkness of night than in the brightness of day. If so, be aware of this fact and remember that the worries of the evening often evaporate with the morning dew.

6. If feelings of hopelessness and anger persist, consult your pastor *and* a physician to gain a greater understanding of the difference between grief and clinical depression.

But I tell you that anyone who is angry
   with his brother is subject to judgment.

Matthew 5:22 NIV

A gentle answer turns away wrath,
   but a harsh word stirs up anger.

Proverbs 15:1 NIV

Do not let the sun go down on your anger,
   and do not give the devil an opportunity.

Ephesians 4:26-27 NASB

Take your burdens of guilt to God
and leave them with God.

Wayne Oates

I am come that they might have life,
and that they might have it
more abundantly.

John 10:10 KJV

Happy is he who does not condemn himself....

—

Romans 14:22 NASB

Chapter 4

GRIEF'S TIMETABLE

The Lord is good to those whose hope is in him, to the one who seeks him; it is good to wait quietly for the salvation of the Lord.

—

Lamentations 3:25-27 NIV

Once grieving begins, almost everyone wonders: "How long will it last?" There is no universal answer to this question. Different people grieve in different ways. You, therefore, will grieve at your own pace.

Mourning is a process that cannot be rushed. Each significant loss is experienced and processed according to its own timetable. But, in the darkness of your own particular sorrow, it is imperative to remember that God is offering His healing hand to you. You, in turn, must extend your hand to Him.

Even devout Christians, even those armed with the healing power of God's Word, must be patient when days and weeks of suffering sometimes turn into months and years. The Psalmist instructs us to *Wait for the Lord; Be strong and let your heart take courage; Yes, wait for the Lord. (Psalm 27:14)* Patience, however, should never be confused with inaction. Although we can never *rush* bereavement, we *can* do our part to face our losses realistically and with a firm trust in God's ability to make us whole once again.

Each of us deals with grief in a different way
and on a different timetable.

Zig Ziglar

To every thing there is a season,
and a time to every purpose under heaven.

Ecclesiastes 3:1 KJV

Patience of spirit is better than
haughtiness of spirit.

Psalm 7: 8 NASB

"GETTING OVER" VERSUS "LIVING AGAIN"

Certain events change our lives forever. The death of a spouse, a child, a close family member, or a loved one makes a permanent mark on the landscape of our lives. Certain tragedies take us to places where we have never been and from which we can never completely return—nor should we wish to: The object of grieving should not be to "get over" the loss of a loved one but instead to incorporate both the love *and* the loss into our hearts...so that we might learn to live again.

Many years after the loss of a loved one, long after we have "processed" our grief and "moved on" with our lives, we may find ourselves reduced to tears at the sight of an old photograph or the first bar of an old, familiar song. Does this mean that we are in some way deficient or that our mourning is somehow incomplete? No. It simply reminds us that some losses stay with us forever and that our loved ones are too important to ever be erased from our hearts. And that's good, because in our hearts—and in God's—is precisely where our loved ones belong. Forever.

My soul waits for the Lord....

Psalm 130: 6 NASB

He gives strength to the weary,
and to him who lacks might He
increases power.

Isaiah 40:29 NASB

Call upon me in the day of trouble:
I will deliver thee, and
thou shall glorify me.

Psalm 50:15 KJV

The Lord who allows each of us to grieve
differently also knows and provides precisely
what will bring comfort to our hearts.

Zig Ziglar

Tribulation brings about perseverance;
and perseverance, proven character,
and character, hope.

Romans 5: 3-4 NASB

The Lord is good, a stronghold in the day
of trouble, and He knows those
who take refuge in Him.

Nahum 1:7 NASB

Sometimes, when I was a child my mother
or father would say, "Shut your eyes and
hold out your hand." That was the promise
of some lovely surprise. I trusted them so
I shut my eyes instantly and held out
my hand. Whatever they were going to give
me I was ready to take. So it should be in
our trust of our heavenly Father. Faith is
the willingness to receive whatever He wants
to give or the willingness not to have what
He does not want to give.

Elisabeth Elliot

In God, whose word I praise, in God I trust;
I will not be afraid.

Psalm 56:4 NIV

Peace I leave with you, my peace I give
unto you; not as the world giveth,
give I unto you. Let not your heart be troubled,
neither let it be afraid.

John 14: 27 KJV

God is our refuge and strength,
a very present help in trouble.

Psalm 46:1 KJV

How do you wait upon the Lord? First you must learn to sit at His feet and take time to listen to His words.

—

Kay Arthur

In thee, O Lord, do I put my trust.

—

Psalm 31:1 KJV

Chapter 5

GOD'S HEALING HAND

For I will restore health unto thee, and I will heal thee of thy wounds, saith the Lord.

—

Jeremiah 30:17 KJV

In time, grief visits everyone: No man or woman, no matter how righteous, is exempt. Christians, however, face their grief with the ultimate armor: God's promises. God's Holy Word does not ensure us freedom from pain, but it tells us that, if we endure, God will be faithful: *For you have need of endurance, so that when you have done the will of God, you may receive what was promised.* (Hebrews 10:36 NASB)

The verses and quotations on the following pages remind us that God stands ready and willing to help heal us if we welcome Him into our hearts. And, the time to welcome Him in is now.

Our healing from grief, to a very great extent,
lies in our daily communication
with the Lord.

Zig Ziglar

O, let the place of secret prayer become
to me the most beloved spot on earth.

Andrew Murray

A true prayer is an inventory of needs,
a catalog of necessities, an exposure of secret
wounds, a revelation of hidden poverty.

C. H. Spurgeon

A STRANGER IN A STRANGE LAND

When Moses fled from the Pharaoh and lived in exile from Egypt, Moses described himself as *a stranger in a strange land. (Exodus 2:22 KJV)* Despite those feelings of loss and alienation, Moses was being prepared by God for a heroic task ahead. When God called Moses out of exile to lead the sons of Israel, Moses was ready for the challenge.

Bereavement is a journey that often leads us to places in our lives that are unfamiliar and frightening. Like Moses, we may feel like strangers in a strange land. In the darkness of our grief, we may feel alone, afraid, and lost. But we are not lost if we depend upon God's ultimate roadmap: His Holy Word.

When we grieve, we are, in a very real sense, exiles from our former selves. We no longer see life in vivid colors but only in muted shades of gray. But just as God prepared Moses during *his* exile, so will God prepare us during ours...if we let Him.

If, in this time of bereavement, you believe that God is finished with you, you are wrong. He has important plans for you still, plans that further the work of His kingdom. God intends that you use this day and the days ahead to seek His will through prayer and through the study of His Word.

Seek God every day and every hour, learning to depend upon His love and grace. Then, when the time is right, God will lead you to the place of His choosing and use you according to the divine wisdom of His plan.

Relying on God has to begin over again every day as if nothing had yet been done.

—

C. S. Lewis

Don't pray when you feel like it;
    make an appointment with the King
        and keep it.

Corrie ten Boom

He who kneels the most stands best.

D. L. Moody

Prayer is God's provision for us to know Him,
    to know His purposes and His ways,
to experience His mighty presence working
    in us and through us to accomplish
        His perfect will.

Henry Blackaby

But if any of you lacks wisdom,
let him ask of God, who gives to all
generously and without reproach,
and it will be given to him.

James 1:5 NASB

The Lord shall give thee rest from thy sorrow,
and from thy fear....

Isaiah 14:3 KJV

Cast thy burden upon the Lord,
and he shall sustain thee:
he shall never suffer the righteous
to be moved.

—

Psalm 55:22 KJV

Lord, I am no longer my own, but Yours.
Put me to what You will, rank me with
whom You will. Let me be employed by You
or laid aside for You, exalted for You
or brought low by You. Let me have all things,
let me have nothing, I freely and heartily
yield all things to Your pleasure and disposal.
And now, O glorious and blessed God, Father,
Son, and Holy Spirit, You are mine and
I am Yours. So be it. Amen.

John Wesley

Begin to know Him now, and finish never.

Oswald Chambers

Let God's promises shine
on your problems.

—

Corrie ten Boom

It is a dreadful truth that the state of having
to depend solely on God is what we all
dread most... It is good of Him to force us;
but dear me, how hard it is for us
to feel that it is good at the time.

C. S. Lewis

For each of us the time is surely coming
when we shall have nothing but God.
Health and wealth and friends and hiding
places will all be swept away, and we shall
have only God. To the man of pseudo-faith
this is a terrifying thought, but
to a person of real faith it is one of
the most comforting thoughts
the heart can entertain.

A. W. Tozer

Blessed are ye that hunger now:
for ye shall be filled. Blessed are ye
that weep now: for ye shall laugh.

Luke 6:21 KJV

I have learned, in whatsoever state I am,
therewith to be content.

Philippians 4:11 KJV

The knowledge that we are never alone calms the troubled sea of our lives and speaks peace to our souls.

—

A. W. Tozer

Are you weak? Weary? Confused?
Troubled? Pressured?
How is your relationship with God?
Is it held in its place of priority?
I believe the greater the pressure,
the greater your need for time
alone with Him.

Kay Arthur

God is light, and in Him
is no darkness at all.

I John 1:5 KJV

I will lift up mine eyes unto the hills, from which cometh my help.

—

Psalm 121:1 KJV

Chapter 6

GOD'S HEALING POWER

Seek the LORD, and his strength:
seek his face evermore.
Remember his marvelous works....

—

Psalm 105:4-5 KJV

Every significant loss carries with it great pain, but grieving Christians can find refuge from their pain through their faith in God. Faith gives assurance in times of doubt; it provides courage during times of fear. During times of intense grief, wise Christians renew themselves through prayer, through worship, and through a careful study of God's Holy Word.

In our darkest moments, we may feel that recovery is impossible, but Jesus reminds us that nothing is too hard for God: *With man this is impossible, but with God all things are possible. (Matthew 19:26 NIV)*

So Christians take heart: *Search for the Lord and for his strength, and keep on searching. Think of the wonderful works he has done, the miracles and the judgments he handed down. (Psalm 105: 4-5 NLT)* No matter your circumstances, no matter your grief, remember that no problem is too big for God. Even yours.

God's heavenly plan doesn't always make earthly sense.

—

Chuck Swindoll

WHY ME?

At times, the world seems to be a terribly unfair place indeed. Why, we ask ourselves, do good people suffer and die? Why are some people seemingly singled out for sickness and pain while others are untouched? Why, we ask, does a righteous and loving God allow such intense pain to come into the lives of His children?

The Book of Job explores the age-old question: "Why do good men and women suffer?" The answer for Job—and for us—is based upon two realities: the finite understanding of man *and* the infinite sovereignty of God. When we question God's purposes and His reasons—or when we try to unravel the puzzle of His mysterious ways—we become frustrated. God alone knows His purposes and plans. In the Biblical record, God never explained His purposes to Job. Neither does He explain Himself to us.

When we mortals suffer profound losses, we cry out, "Why me?" When we do, we are asking the wrong question. Instead, we should ask God,

"What next?" And then, to the best of our abilities and with all of our strength, we should commit ourselves to seek God's will and do His work here on earth.

"Why me?" we ask. That question often remains unanswered *until* God calls us home to a place where our tears—and our questions—are no more.

I am truly grateful that faith enables me
to move past the question of "Why?"

Zig Ziglar

"O the depth of the riches both of
the wisdom and knowledge of God!
How unsearchable are His judgments, and
His ways past finding out!
For who hath known the mind of the Lord?
or who hath been His counselor?"

Romans 11:33-34 KJV

Hope thou in God.

Psalm 42:5 KJV

Sustain me according to Your word,
that I may live; And do not let me be
ashamed of my hope.

Psalm 119:116 NASB

Whoever trusts in the Lord is kept safe.

Proverbs 29:25 NIV

Ask, and it shall be given you;
seek and ye shall find; knock and
it shall be opened unto you.

Matthew 7:7 KJV

Thy faith hath made thee whole.

Mark 5:34 KJV

Faith that hasn't been tested can't be trusted.

Adrian Rogers

God allows us to experience the low points
of life in order to teach us lessons that we
could learn in no other way.

C. S. Lewis

Grief brings us to the point of realizing
the vastness of our love
and God's love for us.

Zig Ziglar

The Lord is my shepherd; I shall not want.
He maketh me to lie down in green pastures:
He leadeth me beside the still waters.
He restoreth my soul: He leadeth me in the
paths of righteousness for His name's sake.
Yea, though I walk through the valley of
the shadow of death, I will fear no evil:
for thou art with me; thy rod and thy staff
they comfort me. Thou preparest a table
before me in the presence of mine enemies:
thou anointest my head with oil;
my cup runneth over. Surely goodness
and mercy shall follow me all the days
of my life: and I will dwell in the house
of the Lord for ever.

—

Psalm 23:1-6

The Lord keeps watch over you
as you come and go, both now and forever.

Psalm 121:8 NLT

Pray, and let God worry.

Martin Luther

Submit each day to God, knowing that
He is God over all your tomorrows.

Kay Arthur

The secret of Christian quietness is not
indifference, but the knowledge that God
is my Father, He loves me, and that
I shall never think of anything He will forget.
Then, worry becomes an impossibility.

Oswald Chambers

Any man can sing in the day....
 It is easy to sing when we can read the notes
  by daylight; but he is the skillful singer who
   can sing when there is not a ray of light
    by which to read....Songs in the night
     come only from God; they are not in
      the power of man.

C. H. Spurgeon

When we cannot see the sunshine
 of God's face, it is blessed to cower down
  beneath the shadow of his wings.

C. H. Spurgeon

When the train goes through a tunnel
 and the world gets dark, do you jump out?
  Of course not. You sit still and trust
   the engineer to get you through.

Corrie ten Boom

Why does God bring thunderclouds and disasters when we want green pastures and still waters? Bit by bit we find, behind the clouds, the Father's feet; behind the lightning, an abiding day that has no night; behind the thunder, "a still small voice" that comforts with a comfort that is unspeakable.

Oswald Chambers

In God's faithfulness lies eternal security.

Corrie ten Boom

When we get to a place where it can't be done unless God does it, God will do it!

Vance Havner

No one yet has ever set out to test God's
promises fairly, thoroughly, and humbly,
and had to report that God's promises don't
work. On the contrary, given a fair
opportunity, God always surprises and
overwhelms those who truly seek
His bounty and His power.

Peter Marshall

Our valleys may be filled with foes and tears;
but we can lift our eyes to the hills to see
God and the angels, heaven's spectators,
who support us according to God's infinite
wisdom as they prepare our welcome home.

Billy Graham

It is a fact of Christian experience that life
is a series of troughs and peaks. In his efforts
to get permanent possession of a soul, God
relies on the troughs more than the peaks.
And some of his special favorites have gone
through longer and deeper troughs
than anyone else.

Peter Marshall

The lives that are getting stronger are
the lives in the desert, deep-rooted in God.

Oswald Chambers

When trials come your way—
as inevitably they will—do not run away.
Run to your God and Father.

Kay Arthur

Snuggle in God's arms.
When you are hurting,
when you feel lonely, left out...
let Him cradle you, comfort you,
reassure you of His all-sufficient
power and love.

—

Kay Arthur

Come unto me, all ye that
labour and are heavy laden,
and I will give you rest.

—

Matthew 11:28 KJV

Chapter 7

LIVING AGAIN

You will show me the way of life,
granting me the joy of your presence
and the pleasures of living
with you forever.

—

Psalm 16:11 NLT

The Book of Ecclesiastes reminds us that there is a time for grief *and* a time for healing. Even if you are currently gripped by an overwhelming sense of loss, rest assured: Better days are ahead. The quality of those days depends, in large part, upon the quality of your relationship with your God and your willingness to make the painful journey through and beyond your bereavement.

If you are grieving, never lose faith in your God or your future. God stands ready to offer His healing hand, so why not take His hand today? And if today, why not now?

Ye shall be sorrowful, but your sorrow
shall be turned into joy.

John 16:20 KJV

Salvation is of the Lord.

Jonah 2:9 KJV

Seek the Lord, and ye shall live....

Amos 5:6 KJV

PERMISSION TO LIVE AGAIN

As you journey through the darkness of your pain, you will, in time, begin to see fleeting glimpses of light. One day, a smile will return to your face, and, for the first time in a long time, you will laugh. As the dawn breaks in your soul and happiness returns to your life, you may feel pangs of guilt. How, you ask, can you ever enjoy life again without your loved one? The answer is as simple as it is Biblical: God intends that your life be one of abundance, not suffering.

Jesus proclaims ...*I am come that they might have life, and that they might have it more abundantly.* (*John 10:10 KJV*) As Christians, we are entitled to the joy that Jesus promises, but to receive it we must open our hands and accept God's healing grace. In the Book of Philippians, Paul states that he has *learned* to be content under any circumstance. (*4:11*) Contentment and joy are as much a part of God's plan for our lives as they were for Paul's life. But, like Paul, we, too, must *learn* the art of contentment.

If you are denying yourself permission to heal, then you are rejecting the abundant life that God intends for you. Don't refuse God's gift.

In the depletion of your spiritual resources, you have the beginnings of new hope: All you need is to feel your need of Him.

—

Wayne Oates

Grief puts us into a position to trust God
alone for our healing and restoration.

Zig Ziglar

When I sit in darkness, the Lord shall be
a light unto me.

Micah 7:8 KJV

He that hath the Son hath life.

I John 5:12 KJV

And let the peace of God rule
in your hearts...
and be ye thankful.

—

Colossians 3:15 KJV

When you and I hurt deeply,
  what we really need is not an explanation
from God but a revelation of God. We need
to see how great God is; we need to recover
  our lost perspective on life. Things get out
    of proportion when we are suffering,
  and it takes a vision of something bigger
    than ourselves to get life's dimensions
        adjusted again.

Warren W. Wiersbe

If we believe in Jesus Christ,
  we can face every problem the world holds.

Oswald Chambers

Even when we cannot see the why
    and wherefore of God's dealings,
we know that there is love in and behind them,
    and so we can rejoice always.

J. I. Packer

God loves you and wants you to experience
    peace and life—abundant and eternal.

Billy Graham

God walks with us....He scoops us up
    in His arms or simply sits with us in silent
strength until we cannot avoid the awesome
recognition that yes, even now, He is there.

Gloria Gaither

The kingdom of God is a kingdom of paradox,
where through the ugly defeat of a cross,
a holy God is utterly glorified. Victory comes
through defeat; healing through brokenness;
finding self through losing self.

Chuck Colsen

He stands fast as your rock, steadfast
as your safeguard, sleepless as your watcher,
valiant as your champion.

C. H. Spurgeon

An infinite God can give all of Himself
to each of His children. He does not
distribute Himself that each may have a part,
but to each one He gives all of Himself
as fully as if there were no others.

A. W. Tozer

These things have I spoken unto you,
　　that my joy might remain in you,
　　and that your joy might be full.

John 15:11 KJV

Let the hearts of those who seek the Lord
rejoice. Look to the Lord and his strength;
　　seek his face always.

I Chronicles 16: 10-11 NIV

To every thing there is a season,
and a time to every purpose
under the heaven...
a time to mourn,
and a time to dance.

—

Ecclesiastes 3:1,4 KJV

Rejoicing is clearly a spiritual command.
To ignore it, I need to remind you,
is disobedience.

Chuck Swindoll

The Lord is glad to open the gate to every
knocking soul. It opens very freely;
its hinges are not rusted, no bolts secure it.
Have faith and enter at this moment
through holy courage. If you knock with
a heavy heart, you shall yet sing with joy of
spirit. Never be discouraged!

C. H. Spurgeon

The grace of God is sufficient
for all our needs,
for every problem
and for every difficulty,
for every broken heart,
and for every human sorrow.

—

Peter Marshall

I approach prayer in a similar way
  as I experience the joy of relationship
with God. No matter how severe "the winter
  of the soul" may have been, standing in
  the presence of God brings pure joy.

Henry Blackaby

Christ alone can bring lasting peace—
  peace with God—peace among men
and nations—and peace within our hearts.

Billy Graham

The ability to rejoice in any situation
  is a sign of spiritual maturity.

Billy Graham

Joy is the serious business of heaven.

C. S. Lewis

This is the day which the Lord hath made;
we will rejoice and be glad in it.

Psalm 118:24 KJV

Therefore do not worry about tomorrow,
for tomorrow will worry about itself.
Each day has enough trouble of its own.

Matthew 6:34 NIV

The LORD is my rock,
and my fortress, and my deliverer;
my God, my strength,
in whom I will trust....

—

Psalm 18:2 KJV

Let not your heart be troubled:
ye believe in God,
believe also in me.

—

John 14:1 KJV

Remember, we go through nothing
  that God does not know about.

Oswald Chambers

Finally, brethren, whatsoever things are true,
  whatsoever things are honest, whatsoever
things are just, whatsoever things are pure,
  whatsoever things are lovely, whatsoever
    things are of good report; if there be
  any virtue, and if there be any praise,
        think on these things.

Philippians 4:8 KJV

I sought the Lord,
and he heard me, and
delivered me from all my fears.

—

Psalm 34:4 KJV

Appendix

THINGS YOU CAN DO

They that sow in tears shall reap in joy.

—

Psalm 126:5 KJV

SLEEP

Periods of grief may result in disturbed sleep or a total lack of sleep. In such cases, consider the following:

1. Reduce your intake of caffeine or eliminate caffeine entirely from your diet. The residual effects of too much coffee or too many soft drinks may be contributing to your sleeplessness.

2. At least one hour before bedtime, begin the process of preparing for sleep by putting yourself into a calmer state. Do not watch television programs that might upset you or "get your juices flowing." Instead, engage in quieter pursuits (such as reading) in order to ready yourself for a good night's sleep.

3. If you cannot fall asleep quickly, do not lay in bed and worry about the fact that you are not sleeping. Get up, pick up a book, and read until you feel tired. Then go back to bed. Your bed should be a place for sleeping, not a place for worrying.

4. Establish regular sleep patterns by getting up at the same time every day. Even if you do not fall asleep until a very late hour, force yourself

out of bed at the same time each morning. This practice will, within a few weeks, help you establish a more normal pattern of sleep. If sleeplessness persists, consult your physician.

5. Troubles and worries are always magnified during the nighttime hours. If you are too worried about a particular topic to fall asleep, do not lay in bed and fret. Instead, get up, take pencil and paper, and write down your worries, along with an action plan to solve them.

6. Engage in sensible physical exercise on a regular basis. Before you begin any new exercise program, consult your physician. Preferably, do not exercise within three hours of bedtime.

7. If you feel that your lack of sleep poses a hazard to your physical or emotional well-being, consult your physician.

8. Create for yourself a sleep-enhancing environment: dark, quiet, comfortable, and cool.

9. Finally, remember the words of Victor Hugo: "Have courage for all the great sorrows of life and patience for the small ones. And when you have finished your daily task, go to sleep. God is awake."

HOLIDAYS AND ANNIVERSARIES

Holidays, anniversaries, weekends, and birth-days are times when memories come flooding back. During these times, you may find yourself dreading the prospect of another "sad day." As these days approach, consider the following:

1. Do not try to gloss over or ignore impor-tant dates. Instead, prepare yourself for the up-coming events by talking about your feelings with family, trusted friends, your pastor, or a counselor.

2. Do not be suprised or upset if a particular holiday or anniversary is a sad occasion. And do not, for a single minute, believe that all future holidays will be lonely. Instead, remind yourself that things will gradually improve with time.

3. If you know a difficult day is looming on the horizon, take the initiative to be with family or friends. Make it *your* responsibility to contact others, do not wait for them to contact you.

4. Do not feel guilty if you enjoy the holiday or anniversary. Your ability to laugh—even if that laughter is mixed with tears—is a sign that heal-ing has begun. Remember that laughter is one of God's gifts.

PUTTING YOUR FEELINGS ON PAPER

You may find it helpful to write down your feelings and memories. Consider the following:

1. You may wish to begin keeping a journal of your thoughts and experiences. As you commit your emotions to paper, you are "working through" your sorrow in a tangible way. Furthermore, you can use your journal as a history of your experiences, thus allowing yourself to gauge the healing that is taking place in your life.

2. You may wish to create a scrapbook of pictures and other reminders of the deceased. The scrapbook is not only a tribute to your loved one, it is also a way of processing your grief.

3. You may wish to compose a letter to the deceased expressing your feelings of love, anger, fear, loss, or hope. This letter may also contain words that you wish you had spoken to the deceased, but did not.

GRIEF VERSUS DEPRESSION

Grief is a natural response to any significant loss. Grief runs its course and gradually lessens over time. Depression, on the other hand, is a physical and emotional condition that is, in almost all cases, treatable by counseling, medication, or both. Left untreated, depression can be extremely dangerous to your physical health and to your emotional well-being.

If you have recently experienced a traumatic loss, grief is unavoidable. But, if you or someone close to you fears that your grief may have evolved into clinical depression, it is time to seek professional help. Consider the following:

1. If you have persistent urges toward self-destructive behavior, or if you feel as though you have lost the will to live, consult a professional counselor or physician immediately.

2. If someone you trust urges you to seek counseling, schedule a session with a professionally trained counselor to evaluate your condition.

3. If you experience persistent and prolonged changes in sleep patterns, or if you experience a significant change in weight (either gain or loss), consult your physician.

4. If you are plagued by consistent, prolonged, severe feelings of hopelessness, consult a physician or professional counselor.

In summary, depression is a serious but treatable condition. If you suspect that depression may have a grip on you or someone you love, seek professional guidance without delay. As the old saying goes: "Better safe than sorry."

FORGIVENESS

Perhaps you are still angry at a loved one who has passed on, or perhaps you still bear a grudge against someone—either alive or dead—who did you great harm. Or perhaps, you have never completely forgiven yourself for some past mistake or failure. If so, it is time to forgive.

God's Word conveys a clear message of forgiveness:

Whenever you stand praying, forgive,
   if you have anything against anyone,
so that your Father in heaven will also forgive
   you your transgressions.

Mark 11:25 NASB

The Bible warns us that the inability to forgive is a spiritual stumbling block. But, because we are human beings, subject to human shortcomings and frailties, forgiveness is difficult.

As you make your journey with God through and beyond your particular grief, you may need to forgive others or you may need to seek forgiveness for yourself. If so, here are some things to consider:

1. Remember that forgiveness is God's way. Acknowledge your own need to forgive others as well as your need, on occasion, to seek forgiveness for yourself. Vow to make forgiveness a part of your spiritual journey with God.

2. Remember that others need not ask for your forgiveness in order for you to forgive them. It takes courage and self-assurance to ask for forgiveness; not everyone is strong enough to ask for it. Forgive them anyway.

3. You may find it helpful to make a written list of those people against whom you still bear bitterness. Then, take that list to God in prayer and continue to do so until you your bitterness is gone.

4. You may experience "relapses" when you again become angry with someone you have already forgiven. If so, do not feel discouraged or guilty; simply take your anger to God in prayer and leave it there. He can handle it.

5. If you remain embittered, or if you are not able to forgive *yourself* for some past failure or mistake, seek the spiritual guidance of your pastor.

MARSHALLING YOUR RESOURCES

As you work through your grief, you will find it helpful to utilize all the resources that are available to you. God intends that you have a meaningful, abundant life, but He expects you to do your part in claiming His blessings. Thus, it is your responsibility to seek out help when you need it. First and foremost, lean upon the love, help, and support of family, friends, fellow church members, and your pastor. Other resources include:

1. Various local counseling services including, but not limited to, pastoral counselors, psychologists, and community mental health facilities.
2. Group counseling programs which may focus on your specific loss. Talking with others who have experienced a loss similar to yours will be extremely helpful.
3. Your personal physician.
4. The local bookstore or library, which will contain specific reading material about your grief and about your particular loss.

FINDING NEW MEANING FOR LIVING

Perhaps your loss has turned your world upside down. Perhaps everything in your life has been changed forever. Perhaps your relationships and your responsibilities have been permanently altered. If so, you may come face-to-face with the daunting task of finding a new purpose for living.

God has an important plan for your life, and part of His plan may well be related to your grief. Your suffering carries with it great potential: the potential for intense personal growth and the potential to help others. As you begin to reorganize your life, always be watchful for ways to use your suffering for the betterment of others. Lend your experienced hand to help fellow travelers, knowing with assurance that the course of your healing will depend upon how quickly you discover new people to help and new reasons to live.

As you make the journey through and beyond your grief, be mindful of this fact: As a wounded survivor, you will have countless opportunities to serve others. And by serving others, you will bring glory to God and meaning to the suffering you have endured.

ABOUT THE AUTHOR

Criswell Freeman is a Doctor of Clinical Psychology who works and lives in Nashville, Tennessee. Dr. Freeman has written over 50 books including two other books on grief:

Your Grief and God's Promises
(Delaney Street Press)

A Time to Grieve, a Time to Heal
(Delaney Street Press)

Dr. Freeman is married, and he has two daughters.